Enabling Distributed Security in Cyberspace

Building a Healthy and Resilient Cyber Ecosystem with Automated Collective Action

March 23, 2011

Enabling Distributed Security in Cyberspace

Building a Healthy and Resilient Cyber Ecosystem with Automated Collective Action

Executive Summary

Like natural ecosystems, the cyber ecosystem comprises a variety of diverse participants – private firms, non-profits, governments, individuals, processes, and cyber devices (computers, software, and communications technologies) – that interact for multiple purposes. Today in cyberspace, intelligent adversaries exploit vulnerabilities and create incidents that propagate at machine speeds to steal identities, resources, and advantage. The rising volume and virulence of these attacks have the potential to degrade our economic capacity and threaten basic services that underpin our modern way of life.

This discussion paper explores the idea of a healthy, resilient – and fundamentally more secure – cyber ecosystem of the future, in which cyber participants, including cyber devices, are able to work together in near-real time to anticipate and prevent cyber attacks, limit the spread of attacks across participating devices, minimize the consequences of attacks, and recover to a trusted state. In this future cyber ecosystem, security capabilities are built into cyber devices in a way that allows preventive and defensive courses of action to be coordinated within and among communities of devices. Power is distributed among participants, and near-real time coordination is enabled by combining the innate and interoperable capabilities of individual devices with trusted information exchanges and shared, configurable policies.

To illuminate such a cyber ecosystem in action, one might look at today's practice known as "continuous monitoring," in which system managers use a variety of software products to automatically detect and report known security vulnerabilities in network nodes. In some cases, system managers further configure their systems to automatically remediate detected security deficiencies. To offer an analogy, continuous monitoring is to a healthy cyber ecosystem as smoke detectors and sprinkler systems are to a "smart" building.

At the other end of sophistication in the orderly management of a complex system, we draw inspiration from the human body's immune system. To paint a picture that mirrors the body's ability to defend itself is complex. It might include layered defenses and countermeasures that work in tandem; specialized roles; powerful methods for rapidly identifying attackers; surge capabilities; and the ability to learn and rapidly adapt. A companion analogy may be made to the public health system and the Centers for Disease Control and Prevention (CDC). Here, cyber equivalent functions might include threat and incident watch, data dissemination, threat analysis, intervention recommendations, and coordination of preventive actions.

Automation is one of three interdependent building blocks of a healthy cyber ecosystem, along with interoperability and authentication. Automation can increase speed of action, optimize decision making, and ease adoption of new security solutions. A healthy cyber ecosystem might employ an automation strategy of fixed, local defenses supported by mobile and global defenses at multiple levels. Such a strategy could enable the cyber ecosystem to sustain itself and supported missions while fighting through attacks. Further, it could enable the ecosystem to continuously strengthen itself against the cyber equivalent of autoimmune disorders.

Interoperability can broaden and strengthen collaboration, create new intelligence, hasten and spread learning, and improve situational awareness. This paper posits three types of interoperability – semantic (i.e., shared lexicon based on common understanding), technical, and policy – as fundamental to integrating disparate cyber participants into a comprehensive cyber defense system. It examines how the cybersecurity community has achieved some early successes by explicitly separating the management of security information from the management of security functions in an approach called security content automation. Such successes include: developing naming conventions and shared lists and catalogs of the fundamental elements that we identify here as the ecosystem; creating and using machine readable languages and formats for expressing security policies or encoding security transactions; and developing and using knowledge repositories for best practices, benchmarks, profiles, standards, templates, checklists, tools, guidelines, rules and principles, among others. The paper also looks at some challenges associated with expanding this approach to ensure a widely distributed, automated, collective defense.

Authentication can improve trust in ways that enhance privacy and decision making. It is integral to many capabilities beyond cyber defense, and the paper looks to the emerging National Strategy for Trusted Identities in Cyberspace (NSTIC), detailed below, to build a shared foundation. The paper calls for identification and authentication technologies that deliver across five operational objectives: security, affordability, ease of use and administration, scalability, and interoperability. Additionally, the paper calls for consumer guides that rate technologies across all five objectives and assist system developers and owners in making phased improvements and selections. For automated cyber defense, it calls for strong standards-based device authentication, including for software, handheld devices, and small, often wireless, devices composing massively scalable grids.

The paper also draws on current research on network-enabled enterprises that is recasting traditional notions of command and control in the direction of focus and convergence. Focus provides the context and defines the purposes of an endeavor, but is agnostic regarding who might be in charge or particular lines of authority. Convergence refers to the goal-seeking process that guides actions and effects, but recognizes that control works in an unconventional manner in highly distributed systems. The paper presents a five-level maturity model for ecosystem focus and convergence that is associated with increasing agility and provides an approach for defining how to achieve and employ these various levels. Ecosystem maturity is further explored through a discussion of healthy attributes—eight for the ecosystem and eighteen for participants and exchanges.

The paper concludes with a brief discussion of incentives and recommendations for the way ahead. It posits that the slow adoption of available best practices and technologies in the face of increasing cyber attacks indicates an imbalance of incentives and proposes that better and more widely disseminated aggregated and anonymized information about the frequency and actual harm of cyber attacks is needed. Despite the many open questions remaining, the field is ripe for planning and action. Feedback on this paper and comment on all aspects of the problem are welcome at cyberfeedback@dhs.gov.

Table of Contents

Background and Purpose

This paper was prepared under the direction of Philip Reitinger, Deputy Under Secretary for the National Protection and Programs Directorate (NPPD), U.S. Department of Homeland Security, with support from the NPPD Cyber+Strategy Staff, the federally funded Homeland Security Systems Engineering and Development Institute (HS SEDI), and the NPPD Office of Cybersecurity and Communications (CS&C). In 2010, NPPD sponsored a government workshop to discuss a draft of this paper. Recommendations from that workshop have been incorporated.

This paper explores a future – a "healthy cyber ecosystem" – where cyber devices collaborate in near-real time in their own defense. In this future, cyber devices have innate capabilities that enable them to work together to anticipate and prevent cyber attacks, limit the spread of attacks across participating devices, minimize the consequences of attacks, and recover to a trusted state.

This paper presents three building blocks as foundational for a healthy cyber ecosystem: automation, interoperability, and authentication. The paper then considers how these building blocks contribute to ecosystem maturity and explores incentives for creating such a system. It concludes with thoughts on the way ahead.

The envisioned end-state is focused specifically on capabilities that can be achieved in the near- and mid-term by utilizing standards-based software and information to strengthen self-defense through automated collective action. This paper is meant to provoke discussion and further exploration of the topic.

The Case for a More Secure Cyber Ecosystem

Cyber attacks have become more frequent, more widespread, and more consequential. Forecasts for 2011 and beyond project continued increases in both the volume and virulence of cyber attacks. These mostly unattributed incidents reduce the availability of this vital medium for information exchange and impair the ability of the information environment to be a mission multiplier and support more effective and efficient business processes. Needless to say, an insecure environment also weakens the privacy of cyber ecosystem participants.

At the same time, the Nation is significantly expanding the cyber capabilities that power its economy and support its homeland and national security. The transformations being undertaken in the financial, health care, energy, transportation, homeland security, defense, and intelligence sectors are predicated on an expectation that cyber devices (computers, software, and communications technologies), communications networks, and embedded control systems for critical infrastructures will be available and perform as expected. (As examples, see Figures 1 and 2 for profiles of The Next Generation Air Transportation System and Smart Grid.)

Cyber defense today is founded on ad hoc, manual processes; yet cyber attacks often follow a well known, systematic escalation path beginning with reconnaissance activities and extending to gaining entry, establishing persistence, setting up external communications pathways, and conducting attack operations. If cyber devices communicated in near real-time with each other about attacks, and took coordinated security-hardening response actions consistent with a defined policy framework, then critical business, mission and privacy objectives could be better supported, and many security risks could be managed proactively and dynamically. Automated defenses could be effective at the earliest, least costly stage of the lifecycle as well as at the later stages of an attack when malicious code and other attack elements propagate at machine speed. These defenses could be effective against all threats including financial fraud, identity theft, and advanced, persistent threats that exploit unauthorized access to intellectual property and sensitive information.

In January 2003, the Slammer worm infected some 247,000 Internet hosts. Over 90

Figure 1: Next Generation Air Transportation System (NextGen)

NextGen is a comprehensive overhaul of U.S. national airspace system from air traffic control to air traffic management and from ground-based to satellite-based capabilities. It is employing continuous roll-out of improvements and upgrades to make air travel more convenient and dependable, more economical, and more environmentally friendly, while ensuring flights are as safe, secure and hassle-free as possible.

NextGen offers advantages to all stakeholders: consumers, service providers, neighbors (e.g., noise reduction), and the environment.

The NextGen portfolio is organized into seven solution sets, each focusing on a series of related operational changes that together will bring about the mid-term system.

The NextGen Information Systems Security Architecture addresses how to:

- Keep the Bad Stuff Out (external boundary protection and certified software management
- Make Sure You Know To Whom You Are Talking (identity and key management)
- If They Get In, Make Sure You Find Them and Deal With the Problem (intrusion detection and response)
- Minimize Damage Once In; Don't Let it Spread (internal policy enforcement)

http://www.faa.gov/nextgen/

Figure 2: Smart Grid

Smart Grid comprises the electric transmission and distribution systems and myriads of local area networks that use distributed energy resources to serve local loads and/or to meet specific application requirements for remote power, village or district power, premium power, and critical loads protection.

Electric grid stakeholders representing utilities, technology providers, researchers, policymakers, and consumers have worked together to define the functions of a smart grid, and they have identified the following characteristics or performance features:

- Self-healing from power disturbance events
- Enabling active participation by consumers in demand response
- Operating resiliently against physical and cyber attack
- Providing power quality for 21st century needs
- Accommodating all generation and storage options
- Enabling new products, services, and markets
- Optimizing assets and operating efficiently

http://www.oe.energy.gov/smartgrid.htm

percent of the infections occurred within 10 minutes of release, and the worm achieved its full scanning rate (over 55 million scans per second) in approximately 3 minutes. While Slammer did not carry a malicious payload, the volume of traffic it produced swamped networks, causing disconnected ATMs (over 13,000 reported by a single bank), cancelled airline flights, and disrupted elections and 911 services. Clean up costs world-wide were estimated at between $750 million and $1.2 billion[12]. Recently, more highly sophisticated and targeted attacks have been regularly reported.

Imagine a future where cyber devices have an innate ability to correlate operational information and to deduce that a device in their domain has been infected with possible malware. One indicator might be an unusually high number of random connection requests and a corresponding high failure rate. The scenario:

- A healthy device detects an infection in another device. (A discussion of healthy participants – persons, devices, and processes – is provided later in this paper);
- The device stops receiving and forwarding messages from the infected source and informs surrounding healthy devices about the identity of the suspected threat;
- Healthy devices receiving the threat alert employ a threshold defense to minimize the risk of false alarms – that is, they defer action until alerts are received from some pre-determined number of independent devices;
- The alert threshold is reached, and participating healthy devices stop receiving and forwarding messages from the infected device, effectively neutralizing its ability to spread the infection; and finally
- Communications are re-established when the infected devices are cleaned.

Some simulations[3][4] indicate that about 30 to 35 percent of devices would need to cooperate in order for such a course of action to work. These numbers are important, because they indicate that success is not dependent on the participation of all or even a majority of devices; therefore, large-scale infrastructure modification is not required to make the ecosystem fundamentally more secure.[5]

The defenses present in a healthy cyber ecosystem could intervene at essentially any point during complex attacks. For example, an alert could come from trusted and authenticated sources such as other devices inside the infrastructure that detect anomalous behavior, another company or entity under attack, a monitoring service, or the United States Computer

---

[1] Sean P. Gorman, Rajendra G. Kulkarni, Larie A. Schintler, and Roger R. Stough, *Least Effort Strategies for Cybersecurity*, http://arxiv.org/ftp/cond-mat/papers/0306/0306002.pdf

[2] Anil Ananthaswamy, *Internet immunity system promises to defang worm attacks*, http://www.newscientist.com/article/mj20327215.000-internet-immune-system-could-block-viruses.html

[3] Gorman et al

[4] Ananthaswamy

[5] See *Using External Security Monitors to Secure BGP*, Patrick Reynolds, Oliver Kennedy, Emin Gun Sirer , and Fred. B. Schneider at http://www.cs.cornell.edu/fbs/publications/NexusBGPtr.pdf for another indicator that ecosystem health could be improved with marginal impact to existing devices, protocols, and operations. Reynolds et al say that deploying an external security monitor to a random 10% of autonomous systems in the Internet suffices to guarantee security for 80% of Internet routes where both endpoints are monitored.

Emergency Readiness Team (US-CERT). If from an external source, the alert could come directly into an entity's systems and in a format such as eXtended Markup Language (XML) that cyber devices could read. In response to the alert, the infrastructure could automatically check itself then notify officials of the exact location and extent of compromise or of susceptibility to a potential attack. In response, a digital policy (i.e., machine instructions) could be deployed to take infected devices offline, change the configuration of healthy devices to harden them against potential attack, block the incoming malware, or block outbound traffic to the receiving site(s). Immediately upon detection of a compromise, a digital policy could be deployed to alert others of the situation and begin sharing discoveries in an information exchange format that could be authenticated and automatically fed into cyber devices in other cyber infrastructures.

A healthy cyber ecosystem would interoperate broadly, collaborate effectively in a distributed environment, respond with agility, and recover rapidly. With a rich web of security partnerships, shared strategies, preapproved and prepositioned digital policies, interoperable information exchanges, and "healthy" participants – persons, devices, and processes – a healthy cyber ecosystem could defend against a full spectrum of known and emerging threats, including attacks against the supply chain, remote network-based attacks, proximate or physical attacks, and insider attacks; improve the reliability and resilience of critical infrastructures; and better assure privacy, business processes, and missions.

Building Blocks for a Healthy Cyber Ecosystem

Building Block 1: Automation

Automated Courses of Action (ACOAs) are strategies that incorporate decisions made and actions taken in response to cyber situations. Automation frees humans to do what they do well – think, ask questions, and make judgments about complex situations. Automation allows the speed of response to approach the speed of attack, rather than relying on human responses to attacks that are occurring at machine speed. With the ability to execute at machine speed, defenders could get inside the turning circles or decision cycles of attackers. Further, automation could make it easier to adopt and adapt new or proven security solutions.

One potential inspiration for ACOAs is the human immune system, illustrated in Figure 3.[6]

---

[6] See "Immunology, diversity, and homeostasis: the past and future of biologically inspired computer defenses, Anil Somayaji, Journal Information Security Tech., Vol 12, Issue 4. September 2007, *http://portal.acm.org/beta/citation.cfm?id=1324630*, for a useful survey of this field.

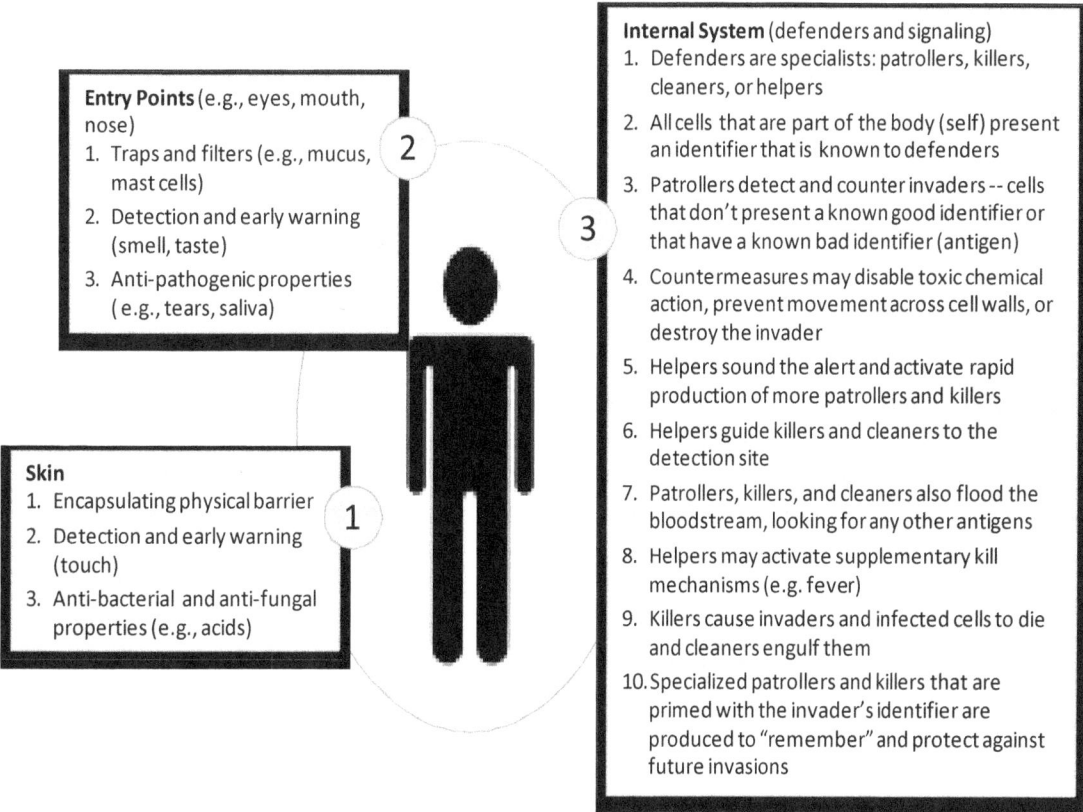

Figure 3: Overview of Human Immune System

Entry Points (e.g., eyes, mouth, nose)
1. Traps and filters (e.g., mucus, mast cells)
2. Detection and early warning (smell, taste)
3. Anti-pathogenic properties (e.g., tears, saliva)

Skin
1. Encapsulating physical barrier
2. Detection and early warning (touch)
3. Anti-bacterial and anti-fungal properties (e.g., acids)

Internal System (defenders and signaling)
1. Defenders are specialists: patrollers, killers, cleaners, or helpers
2. All cells that are part of the body (self) present an identifier that is known to defenders
3. Patrollers detect and counter invaders -- cells that don't present a known good identifier or that have a known bad identifier (antigen)
4. Countermeasures may disable toxic chemical action, prevent movement across cell walls, or destroy the invader
5. Helpers sound the alert and activate rapid production of more patrollers and killers
6. Helpers guide killers and cleaners to the detection site
7. Patrollers, killers, and cleaners also flood the bloodstream, looking for any other antigens
8. Helpers may activate supplementary kill mechanisms (e.g. fever)
9. Killers cause invaders and infected cells to die and cleaners engulf them
10. Specialized patrollers and killers that are primed with the invader's identifier are produced to "remember" and protect against future invasions

The internal system is actually two interrelated systems: one that is stationary and local to cells (cell mediated) and one that is global to the entire body, moving throughout it via the bloodstream and lymph systems (humoral). Each of these interrelated systems has its own locus for sustainment (e.g., thymus, bone marrow) and sophisticated mechanisms for synchronized activity.[7][8]

A healthy cyber ecosystem might employ an automation strategy of fixed local defenses supported by mobile and global defenses at multiple levels. Such a strategy could enable the cyber ecosystem to sustain itself and supported missions while fighting through attacks. Further it could enable the ecosystem to continuously strengthen itself against the cyber equivalent of autoimmune disorders. For example, within an organization, cyber devices that directly provide end user, mission, or business functionality might maintain a high awareness of user behavior, expectations, and service level agreements, be tuned to sense and respond to user situations, signal local or user level status to organizational devices, and correlate discoveries and synchronize responses with organizational devices.

---

[7] *Human Physiology/The Immune System,* http://en.wikibooks.org/wiki/Human_Physiology/The_Immune_System
[8] *How Your Immune System Works,* http://health.howstuffworks.com/immune-system.htm

Cyber devices that provide or manage organization-wide connectivity and services might be tuned to sense and respond to organizational situations, signal organizational status to user level devices, correlate discoveries and synchronize responses with user level devices, and provide support or augmentation to user situations. Enforcement of organizational policies such as privacy protection could be synchronized across user and organizational levels.

In addition to the ability to signal and synchronize across levels, each level could have internal synchronization and analysis capabilities. For example, all devices supporting users, or classes of users, could share a focus and convergence approach that would include security policies and pooled analytic resources, as could all devices supporting organizational services or classes of services. In turn, an organization could share information and coordinate activities or synchronize ACOAs with a larger business, political, or geographic domain, or with the world-wide cyber environment.

Cyber devices endowed with strong feed forward and feedback signaling mechanisms that assume and can accommodate communications failures and operating in an environment with trusted end-to-end identification and authentication of all participants would enjoy a heightened ability to observe, record, and share what is happening to and around them. In turn, they could:

- Proactively take preventive measures;

- Reject requests that do not fit the profile of what is good, *a priori*, for themselves or the larger cyber environment;

- Sense malicious actors and autonomously refine the evidence captured for diagnosis or in support of the development of future prevention methods; and

- Autonomously enact defensive responses or even build such responses in real time.[9]

A companion source of inspiration for ACOAs comes from the public health sector, although for many processes in this domain, automation is some distance away. Public health services conduct population health surveillance and react to threats to the overall health of communities. The stated mission of the Centers for Disease Prevention and Control (CDC) is: "to collaborate to create the expertise, information, and tools that people and communities need to protect their health – through health promotion, prevention of disease, injury and disability, and preparedness for new health threats."[10] The cyber equivalent of a CDC might perform functions such as the following:

- Watch: Gather data on cyber threats and cybersecurity outbreaks that are analogous to the information about diseases reported by health care providers.

- Data dissemination: Provide data about the spread and danger of threats to help communities and organizations plan protective measures and responses.

[9] Cyber Leap Year Summit Co-Chairs' Report,
http://www.cyber.st.dhs.gov/docs/National_Cyber_Leap_Year_Summit_2009_Co-Chairs_Report.pdf
[10] The CDC Mission, http://www.cdc.gov/about/organization/mission.htm

- Cyber threat analysis: Investigate and diagnose cyber threats in the community. Where possible, verify outbreaks of new cyber-threats and understand the causes, extent and impact of these outbreaks.

- Intervention analysis and recommendations: Provide a cost/benefit analysis of potential interventions and make recommendations.

- Coordination of preventive actions: Coordinate response strategies and their execution, for example, the equivalent of quarantining and vaccination strategies or cyber patrolling for fraud.[11]

Building Block 2: Interoperability

Interoperability allows cyber communities to be defined by policies rather than by technical constraints and permits cyber participants to collaborate seamlessly and dynamically in automated community defense. Interoperability enables common operational pictures and shared situational awareness to emerge and disseminate rapidly. The creation of new kinds of intelligence (such as fused sensor inputs), coupled with rapid learning at both the machine and the human levels, could fundamentally change the ecosystem.

Unfortunately, within cybersecurity today, many available devices (e.g., firewalls, file integrity checkers, virus scanners, intrusion detection systems, anti-malware software) operate independently and neither exchange data nor have consistent security policies. Each of them may have been developed by a different vendor, perhaps even competitors, without adherence to internationally accepted open standards. In other cases, the standards are not yet mature. Thus, in today's ecosystem, collaboration is possible but difficult. We must reach a point where the only barriers to collaboration across devices, people, and organizations are those we choose to impose by policy, not those that are imposed on us by technology.

Three types of interoperability[12] are fundamental to integrating the many disparate participants into a comprehensive cyber defense system that can create new intelligence and make and implement decisions at machine speed:

- **Semantic Interoperability.** The ability of each sending party to communicate data and have receiving parties understand the message in the sense intended by the sending party.

---

[11] An approach that is also inspired by public health models is described in *Collective Defense: Applying Public health Models to the Internet* http://www.microsoft.com/mscorp/twc/endtoendtrust/vision/internethealth.aspx. In this approach, access to other online resources is contingent upon the health of a device. Devices seeking access must be able to demonstrate good health through a trusted health certificate. If the device's health level is acceptable, then access is granted. If a security concern is identified, then the entity being petitioned for access (an Internet Service Provider, for example) could provide a notice that assists the user in addressing the security concern, render advice or assistance, or direct the user to resources for remediation.

[12] National Strategy for Trusted Identities in Cyberspace (NSTIC)

- **Technical Interoperability.** The ability for different technologies to communicate and exchange data based upon well defined and widely adopted interface standards.

- **Policy Interoperability.** Common business processes related to the transmission, receipt, and acceptance of data among participants.

Within cybersecurity, all three types of interoperability are being enabled through an approach that has been refined over the past decade by many in industry, academia, and government. It is an information-oriented approach, generally referred to as [cyber] *security content automation* and comprises the following elements.[13]

- **Enumerations.** These are lists or catalogs of the fundamental entities of cybersecurity, for example, cyber devices and software items (CPE); device and software configurations (CCE); publicly known weaknesses in architecture, design, or code (CWE); publicly known flaws or vulnerabilities (CVE); or publicly known attack patterns (CAPEC). Enumerations enable semantic interoperability.

- **Languages and Formats.** These incorporate enumerations and support the creation of machine-readable security state assertions, assessment results, audit logs, messages, and reports. Examples include patterns associated with assets, configurations, vulnerabilities, and software patches (XCCDF & OVAL); security announcements (CAIF), events (CEE), malware (MAEC); risk associated with vulnerability (CVSS), sensor collection and correlation (ARF), and US-CERT security bulletins and incident reports (NIEM). Languages and formats enable technical interoperability.

- **Knowledge Repositories.** These contain a broad collection of best practices, benchmarks, profiles, standards, templates, checklists, tools, guidelines, rules, and principles, among others. In many respects, knowledge repositories serve as the cybersecurity community "memory" and enable policy interoperability. Examples include Information Assurance Checklists housed on the National Checklist Program website (http://checklists.nist.gov/), Department of Defense Security Technical Implementation Guides (STIGs), and vendor guides."

Figure 4 presents a history of U.S. Government supported security content automation efforts along with projected achievements through 2014. Projections are based on current resourcing and the interests of a largely volunteer and self-directed community. Figure 4 also illustrates how standards build upon themselves to expand functionality over time (e.g., the expansion of configuration management capabilities from desktops to networks).

---

[13] See the Glossary at the end of this paper for the full name of the various named standards.

Figure 4. History and Near Term Forecast of Cyber Security Automation Standards Development Activity

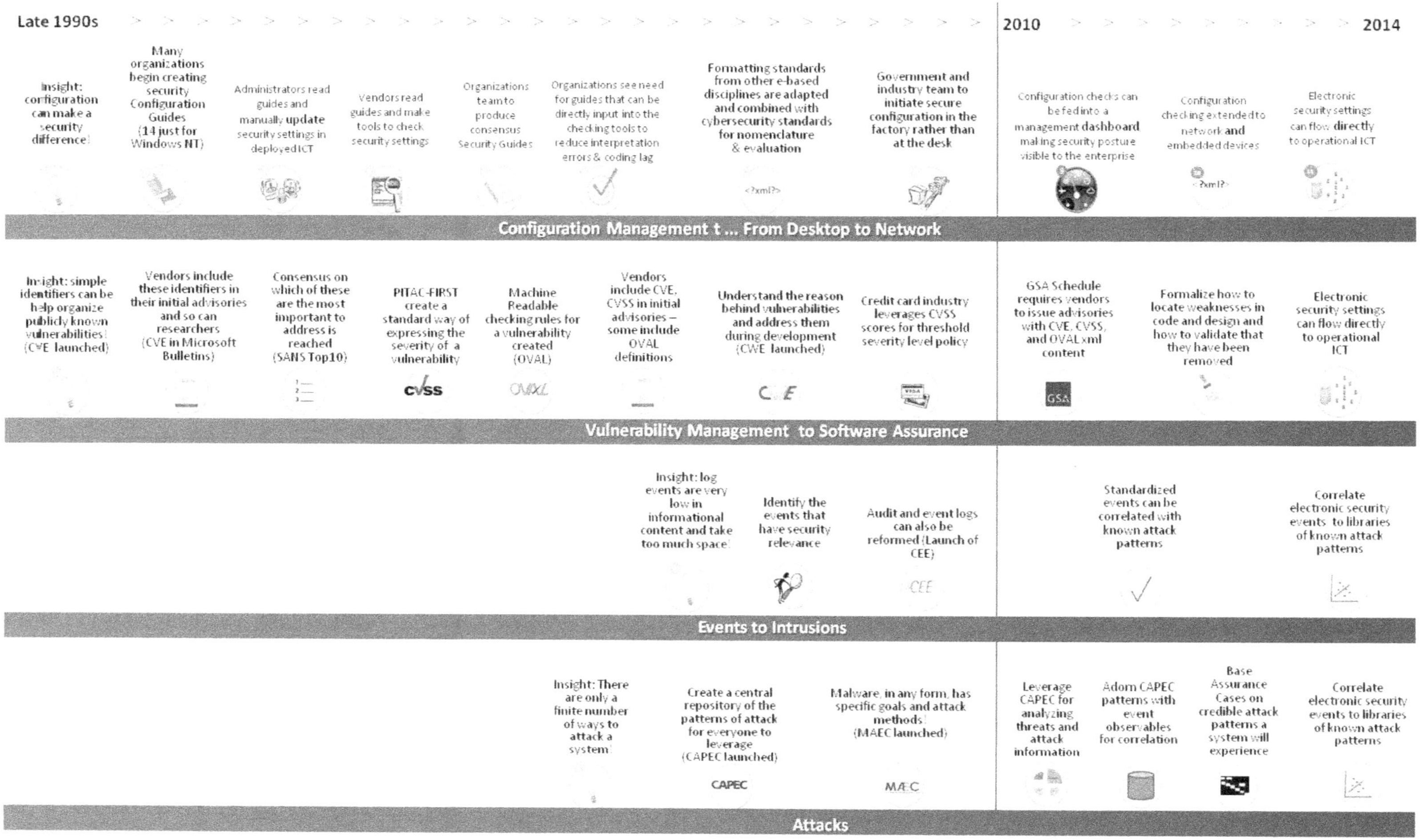

Another way to approach the evolution of cyber security content automation is through a strategic consideration of what is needed and possible. Figure 5 presents an array of security functions that can be transformed by content automation and exchange. Standards supporting the first wave are extant and documented in NIST SP 800-126, The Technical Specification for the Security Content Automation Protocol[14]. Many of the standards necessary to support the second wave are in development now, and some of the challenges associated with bridging the two waves are discussed later in this section. The third wave identifies a logical progression. As with the historical transition from e-commerce to e-business, succeeding waves build in capability and become more strategic in focus.

Figure 5: Strategic Consideration of Cyber Security Content Automation

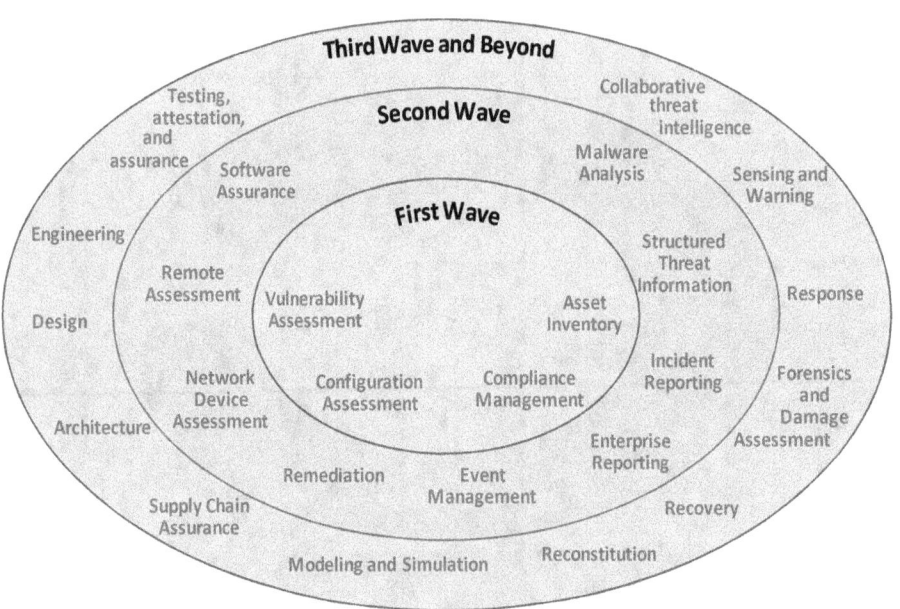

The success of any single function and the integration of functions within and across waves depend on semantic, technical, and policy interoperability. These three types of interoperability are themselves interdependent, and they mature as each adapts to changes in the other. Some level of semantic interoperability must be achieved and some vision of policy (or process) interoperability is necessary in order to successfully develop and employ technical interoperability. A simple example would be the publication of US-CERT bulletins in XML blobs. The technical standards must be underpinned by sender/receiver agreement on the meaning of the content and by agreement on how the XML-structured bulletins are to be received and processed. In turn, achievements in technical interoperability enable advances in semantic and policy interoperability, and these advances trigger further advances in technical interoperability.

---

[14] NIST SP 800-126 Rev 1, DRAFT *The Technical Specification for the Security Content Automation Protocol (SCAP): SCAP Version 1.1, January 11, 2011* , http://csrc.nist.gov/publications/PubsSPs.html

Advances in semantic and policy interoperability almost always start with persons and progress to devices. Further, advances in interoperability have short-term advantages. For example, the first wave of security content automation is enabling the recent federal commitment to continuous monitoring, and progress in the second wave, combined with gains achieved during the first wave, is enabling XML-based incident reporting to the US-CERT.

The three waves of automated security functions depicted in Figure 5 can be summarized as progress along three axes:

Figure 6: Axes of Progress

Axis	Progression
Space	From hosts to networks and applications
Time	From static to dynamic
Capability	From configuration to integrated policy and audit

A third way to examine cyber security content automation is through the generalized functional model in use by the standards community. As illustrated in Figure 7 below, the security functions contained in this model generally represent the first wave plus a portion of the second wave. Security content automation standards that can facilitate the exchange of information with and among functions are annotated adjacent to each function, input, or output.

Figure 7: Generalized Functional Model Informing Standards Development

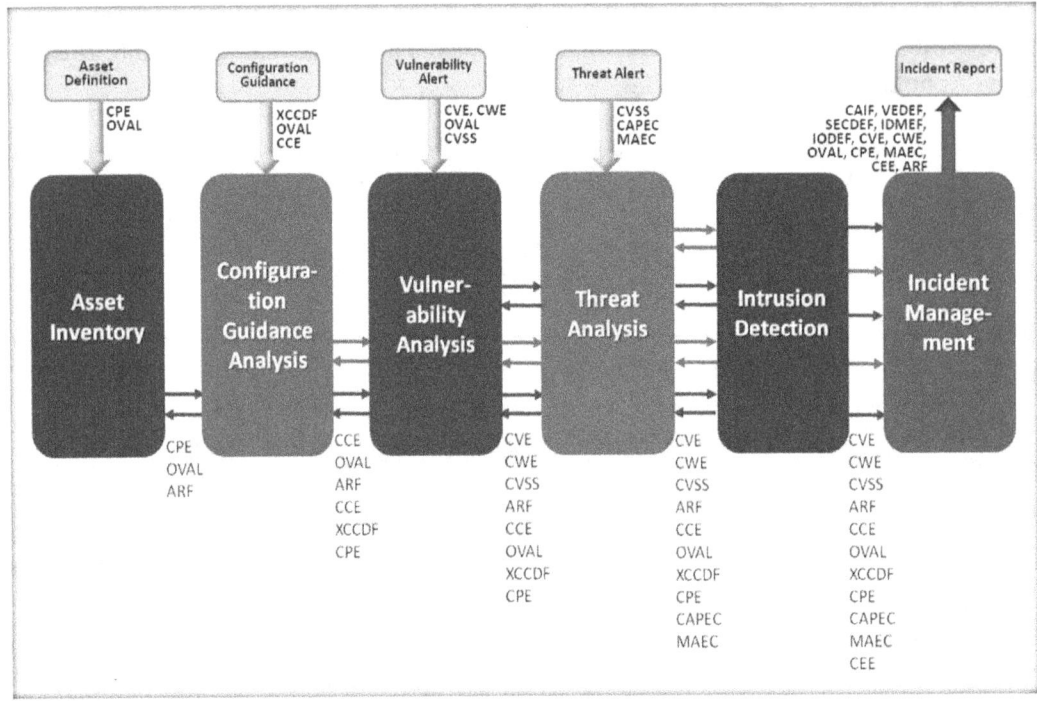

This model is lifecycle-oriented and enterprise- or organization-focused. Capabilities are expected to build on one another (from left to right). Each function (e.g., asset inventory, configuration guidance analysis, vulnerability analysis) is viewed as a black box and assumed to be provided by current or future commercial products. Integration across functions is also assumed. The current model does not address formulation or dynamic evolution of ACOAs; however, it does provide a reasonable foundation for ACOA execution.

In general, the functions can be organized into "pre-incident detection" (asset inventory, configuration guidance analysis, and vulnerability analysis plus threat analysis) and "post-incident detection" (intrusion detection and incident management plus threat analysis). This organizing construct aligns with the waves presented in Figure 5 above. As illustrated, the structuring of threat information is a second wave activity. The effort to standardize threat alerts and automate threat analysis may prove more complex than previous security content automation efforts because standardization must:

- Bridge these two operational dimensions (pre- and post- incident detection); and

- Add value for enterprises that lack automated capabilities on one side or the other.

In addition, on the whole, the "post-incident detection" space is less standards-based than the "pre-incident detection" space. Advances in semantic and policy interoperability regarding what constitutes a reportable incident, what attributes best support incident management, and how these attributes are to be sourced and shared are needed to advance technical standards and interoperability.

Building Block 3: Authentication

Authentication should enable trusted online decisions. Nearly every decision in an online environment involves resources and actors at a distance. When needed for a decision, authentication provides appropriate assurance that the participants are authentic or genuine, and it should do so in a way that enhances individual privacy. In a healthy ecosystem, authentication could extend beyond persons to include cyber devices (e.g., computers; software, or information).

Authentication is critical to cyber defense because communications and content attribution are essential factors in security decisions. Authentication is also foundational to many capabilities beyond cyber defense.[15]

In a healthy cyber ecosystem, sending and receiving parties could be known and accountable for their actions, but protect anonymity where it may be needed to preserve the purpose of the exchange. Consumers of shared cyber awareness could judge the trustworthiness of providers and their contributions, and providers could confirm that requesters are authorized access to such information. Authentication mechanisms could be strong enough to protect against identity theft and spoofing, while at the same time remain affordable, easy to use and administer, scalable, and interoperable. They could also be designed to enhance individual privacy by allowing voluntary, opt-in regimes.

Common authentication technologies rely on (1) something you know (e.g., passwords), (2) something you have (e.g., digital credential), or (3) something you are (e.g., biometrics). Each of these technologies has characteristics that impact security strength, affordability, ease of use and administration, scalability, and interoperability. Significant considerations include ease of integration into emerging and deployed devices and software applications and ease of exchange or federation across networks and organizations.

Unfortunately, in today's market, system developers and owners find few if any technologies that deliver on all five operational objectives: security, affordability, ease of use and administration, scalability, and interoperability. The usual approach is to divide up enterprises and use populations to control and vary the objective that gets optimized. This creates a complex landscape of multiple authentication technologies with limited interoperability, vulnerable security seams, and barriers to business or organizational change.

A healthy cyber ecosystem could have standards-based authentication technologies that deliver more comprehensively across all five operational objectives. To support near-term decisions, consumer guides that rate technologies across all five objectives and assist system developers and owners in making phased improvements and selections could be available. For automated

---

[15]. For additional detail, see the National Strategy for Trusted Identities in Cyberspace, available at http://www.dhs.gov/xlibrary/assets/ns_tic.pdf

cyber defense, a healthy cyber ecosystem could have strong standards-based device authentication, including small and usually wireless devices composing massively scalable grids. Finally, a healthy ecosystem could have broad ways to express and manage trust that combine trust attributes about people, transactions, technology, and information into new decision frameworks and metrics. Such frameworks could recognize that trust is not a binary or static state, but is fluid and conditioned upon evolving operational and environmental factors.

Key Concepts

Focus, Convergence, and Maturity

The prevailing construct for cybersecurity is illustrated in Figure 8. Cybersecurity processes are a combination of local and global activities. The distribution of activities between local and global may differ from process to process, activity to activity, participant to participant, or event to event. The range of local-to-global extends from the circuitry within a single cyber device (e.g., a mobile phone, personal computer, medical device, or electric grid component) to distributed software applications, data centers, networks, and clouds. To successfully defend against active and intelligent adversaries in such complex and uncertain networked environments, current thinking suggests the need for a new view of command and control, one that emphasizes agility, focus, and convergence:

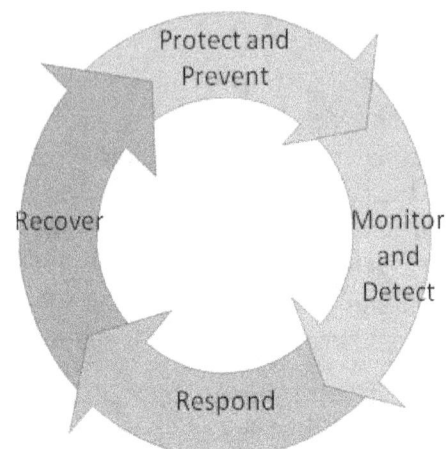

Figure 8. Prevailing Cybersecurity Construct

> In brief, agility is the critical capability that organizations need to meet the challenges of complexity and uncertainty; focus provides the context and defines the purposes of the endeavor; convergence is the goal-seeking process that guides actions and effects. …. Focus as a replacement for command speaks directly to what command is meant to accomplish while being agnostic with respect to the existence of someone in charge or particular lines of authority. Similarly, convergence speaks directly to what control (the verb) is meant to achieve without asserting that control as a verb is possible or desirable.[16]

As suggested earlier, this paper focuses primarily on how networked devices can become actors in their own and the network's defense. To illustrate a range of capabilities that such devices

---

[16] Agility, Focus, and Convergence: The Future of Command and Control, David S. Alberts (OASD-NII), The International C2 Journal, Vol 1, No 1, 2007, http://www.dodccrp.org/files/IC2J_v1n1_01_Alberts.pdf

will begin to embody, we present a five-level maturity model in Figure 9.[17] The model considers Focus and Convergence (F&C) in terms of increasing agility, that is, effectiveness in dealing with change over time. As with other maturity models, Level 5 represents the highest level of focus and convergence, while Level 1 represents the lowest. The five-level model is not a normative scale. That is, Level 5 is not always better than Level 3. Communities may opt to operate at lower levels for reasons of cost, efficiency, or other reasons. Describing the ecosystem in terms of multiple levels helps illustrate and demonstrate a system's high tolerance for diversity, as different communities will inevitably have different needs and be in different stages of evolution at any given point in time. For example, there are a number of outdated system components within the nation's critical infrastructure that are not able to interface with modern systems but will remain an important part of the ecosystem in the near term. The ability to leap-frog from this legacy technology to a modern cyber infrastructure is something that should be explored.

Figure 9: Focus and Convergence Maturity Model for Networked Environments

F&C Maturity Levels		
Level 5	Edge F&C	Characterized by a robustly-networked collection of devices having widespread and easy access to information, sharing information extensively, interacting in a rich and continuous fashion, and having the broadest possible distribution of decision rights. The objective of Edge F&C is to enable the community to self-synchronize in an agile and adaptable manner.
Level 4	Collaborative F&C	Characterized by multiple devices working together toward a common purpose and under a single, shared plan. Involves a considerable delegation of decision rights to the community. Aims to develop synergies by negotiating and establishing shared intent as well as a shared security policy, establishing or reconfiguring roles, coupling actions, and by engendering a rich sharing of resources and awareness.
Level 3	Coordinated F&C	Characterized by multiple devices related by mutual support for intent, expressed as links between and among security policies and actions that reinforce and enhance effects along with some pooling of resources for specified activities.
Level 2	De-conflicted F&C	Characterized by a partitioning of the problem space among devices to avoid adverse cross-effects. Establishment and maintenance of the partitions requires limited information

---

[17] Adapted from the North Atlantic Treaty Organization (NATO) Network Enabled Capability (NEC) C2 Maturity Model, February 2010 , www.dodccrp.org

F&C Maturity Levels		
		sharing and interaction among devices.
Level 1	Isolated F&C	Characterized by individual devices exercising focus and convergence only over their own resources. Hence, there is no shared objective; neither is there information distribution nor any other interaction among devices.

To consider how such a model might be applied, a framework for defining and thinking about the space of all possible F&C approaches is helpful. Three variables define the essence of F&C, and thus the F&C Approach Space is illustrated in Figure 10 below.

Figure 10: Focus and Convergence (F&C) Approach Space[18]

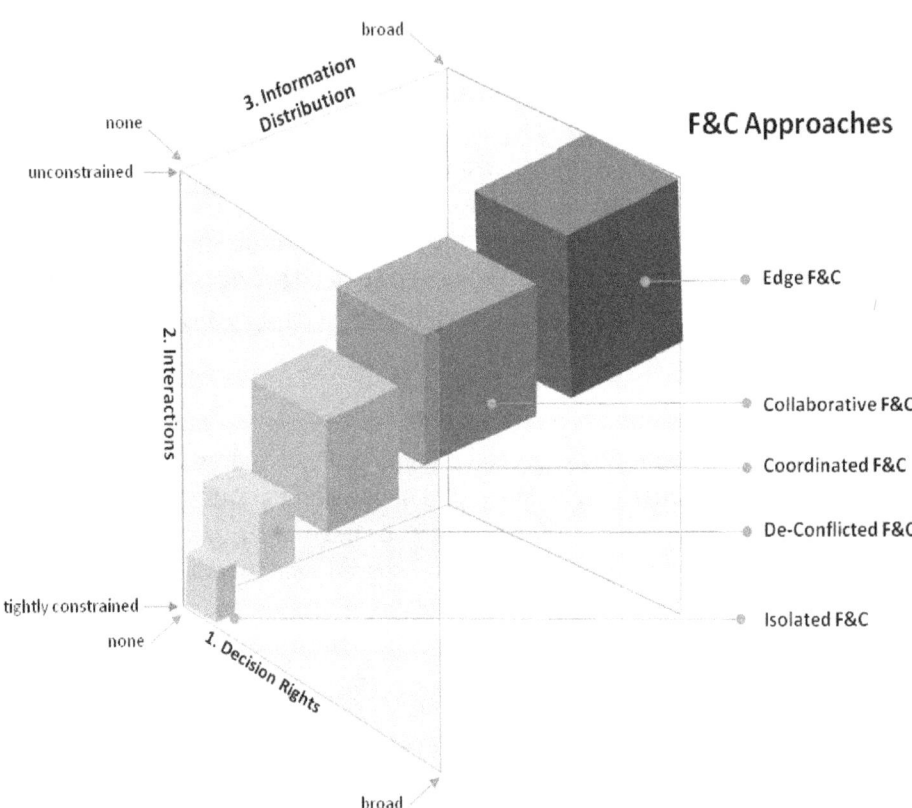

As Figure 10 illustrates, any focus and convergence approach may be viewed as a function of three interrelated dimensions:

1. The allocation of decision rights to the community;

---

[18] NATO NEC C2 Maturity Model

2. The patterns of interaction that take place between and among devices; and

3. The distribution of information among devices.

Figure 11 summarizes how these three dimensions vary among the F&C levels.

Figure 11: Dimensions of Focus and Convergence[19]

F&C Approach	Allocation of Decision Rights to the Collective	Patterns of Interaction Among Participating Devices	Distribution of Information
Edge F&C	Not explicit, Self-Allocated (Emergent, Tailored, and Dynamic)	Unlimited as Required	All relevant available information is accessible
Collaborative F&C	Joint or Combined Process and Single Shared Security Policy	Significant Broad	Organic Information plus Information across Collaborative Areas and Functions
Coordinated F&C	Mutual Review Process and Linked Security Policies	Limited and Focused	Organic Information plus Information about Coordinated Areas and Functions
De-Conflicted F&C	Established Constraints	Very Limited Sharply Focused	Organic Information plus Information about Constraints and Seams
Isolated F&C	None	None	Organic Information

(F&C Agility increases from bottom to top)

Increased agility (moving from the bottom left to top right within the F&C approach space in Figure 10) can be viewed as:

- The ability of devices to adopt ever wider ranges of approaches;

- The ability of devices to recognize and adopt an appropriate approach, which is determined by the nature of the situation and how it is likely to evolve; and

- The ability of devices to change approaches if necessary in a timely manner.

Considering F&C within an approach space also supports a growing recognition that there may be no single best system design or configuration, no best process for all situations and circumstances. Rather than optimization, the uncertainty in the mission space combined with the diverse and interacting effects of countermeasures and the complexity inherent in collective action lead to a need for agility. This might mean that devices routinely operate at lower levels of F&C for economy but have the ability to switch to higher levels of F&C for selected situations. It might also mean that routine F&C levels vary by devices' roles or locations within the ecosystem.

---

[19] NATO NEC C2 Maturity Model

Increased agility among cyber devices is necessarily dependent upon and exists in synchrony with the agility of the organizations that own and operate them and the business or mission processes that consume their services. The three building blocks described earlier – automation, authentication and interoperability – increase agility and enable collective cyber defense. Decision rights originate with persons, organizations and business processes; and interoperability ensures that any delegation to cyber devices is communicated in a way that both humans and machines can understand. Automation provides the ability to act upon delegated decision rights at machine speed, and authentication allows the data necessary for a given decision to be trusted.

Attributes of a Healthy Cyber Ecosystem

Looking at the ecosystem through building blocks and maturity levels helps envision how a healthy ecosystem might work and how it might self-defend through automated collective action. This section begins to examine the desired end-state. What might be different in a healthy ecosystem? What might be the value added?

In a healthy cyber ecosystem, we might find:

- **Information connected across space and time**. Information discovered or created in one part of the ecosystem conveys rapidly to others rather than being siloed, e.g., information is preserved in ways that help discover patterns over time and can be configured to protect Personally Identifiable Information (PII) and other sensitive data.

- **Rapid and essentially universal learning**. Machines learn from each other and people learn from machines.

- **Greater attribution**. Machines and humans work together to improve attribution where needed while enhancing privacy.

- **New analytics**. Data from multiple, otherwise discrete sources (e.g., sensors, red teams, trouble tickets) are fused, aggregated or otherwise transformed to create new intelligence.

- **Greater network reach**. Security content is separated from delivery mechanisms and managed as an ecosystem asset. Earlier research in Tailored Trustworthy Spaces[20] results in powerful new ways to work across multiple trust or classification levels.

- **New defensive tactics**. Earlier research in Moving Target Defense[21], combined with shared security policies and new intelligence, enables new courses of action such as dynamic networking or uncertainty. In other words, attacks only work once (i.e. one victim or one device) if at all.

---

[20] Federal Cybersecurity Game-change Research and Development (R&D) Themes, http://cybersecurity.nitrd.gov/page/federal-cybersecurity-1

[21] Federal Cybersecurity Game-change Research and Development (R&D) Themes

- **Lifecycle Feedback.** Rich feedback loops from operations into the front end of system and technology life cycles reduce costs, shorten adoption cycles, and improve ecosystem health.

Another way to examine the desired end state is through the qualities or attributes the building blocks might help create. A healthy cyber ecosystem might be:

- **Inclusive.** Encompassing capabilities embedded in an ever-widening web that extends far beyond traditional notions of the public Internet or of information technology (IT) and services. A healthy cyber ecosystem would include the Smart Grid with its energy-controlled home networks and IP addressable appliances, the next generation of the National Airspace System which takes advantage of satellite capabilities, and the large number of legacy devices and control systems which must interoperate with the newest technologies.

- **Effective.** Able to defend against all types of cyber threats, including supply chain attacks; remote or network-based attacks, including those launched by sophisticated and well-resourced attackers using persistent methods; proximate or physical attacks or adverse events; and insider or disgruntled employee attacks.

- **Smart.** Able to sense the environment, recognize patterns, and share information in near-real time across sectors and communities at both the human and machine levels in order to assure authorized transactions, prevent the most serious security breaches and increase response effectiveness when breaches or other adverse events do occur.

- **Barrier-free.** Having security choices instantiated in configurable digital policies rather than being "hardwired" in network or system designs or imposed by technology limitations or shortfalls. Designers would design with the assumption that everything will be shared with everyone, and the only barriers to collaboration would be those imposed by policy.

- **Optimized.** Having capabilities and decision making allocated among humans and machines so as to best leverage the strengths and cycle-times of each, consistent with maintaining agility. Further, having cyber defense organized so that machines defend against machines and people defend against people.

- **Understandable.** Having security expressed in user or stakeholder terms rather than in specialized security "jargon" and recognizing that everyone is a cybersecurity stakeholder. For example, stakeholders might want global visibility into the cyber environment, the ability to query the environment and get back a high fidelity answer, and the ability to rationalize security costs.

- **Assured.** Able to sustain consumer confidence over time. This might mean moving beyond traditional security notions of "preventing unwanted transactions" to "ensuring the right transactions occur," which could contribute more broadly to a sense of consumer safety and trust in sector operations for transportation, energy, health, etc.

- **Usable**. Having assembly, configuration, operational, and performance properties that are straightforward and well-behaving, rather than overwhelmingly complicated, brittle, and error-prone.

Attributes of Healthy Participants

Just as healthy individuals are essential to healthy communities, healthy participants are essential to a healthy cyber ecosystem. Cyber ecosystem participants include persons (both individuals and entities), devices, and processes.

Persons who are "unhealthy" cyber participants might lack awareness or skills, or they may not be who they claim. Persons who are "healthy" cyber participants might have continuing access to a range of education, training and awareness opportunities, including but not limited to exercises, simulations, and fully-immersive learning environments. Further, they might have validated skills that have been codified for their occupations or positions and strongly proofed cyber identities.

"Unhealthy" cyber devices (computers, software, and communications technologies) lack awareness, functionality, or capacity or feature purposeful deceptions. "Healthy" cyber devices are:

- **Self Aware**. Having the ability to collect information about security properties, draw conclusions, and report or act upon the conclusions.

- **User Aware**. Having the ability to collect or receive and process information about supported users, missions, or business processes or assigned role in a larger cyber infrastructure plus ability to draw conclusions, report or act upon the conclusions, and implement policies that assure user privacy.

- **Environmentally Aware**. Having the ability to collect or receive and process information about the security of surrounding cyber devices of interest or the cyber environment, draw conclusions, and report or act upon the conclusions.

- **Smart**. Having the ability to retrospectively examine events and associated responses, correlate historical patterns with current status data, and either select from a range of ACOAs or formulate a new ACOA. Examples of ACOAs that may be deployed in near-real time include filtering or re-routing traffic, cordoning off portions of the network or applications, changing access levels, reconfiguring assets, and quarantining users.

- **Autonomously Reacting**. Having the ability to initiate an ACOA.

- **Dynamic.** Having the ability to alter appearance or persona. Ideally, alterations are enacted on cycle times that are shorter than target acquisition and attack execution times. For example, today's systems tend to rely on selected system parameters for security, such as duration of timeouts or corruption thresholds. Typically, these parameters are chosen in advance and fixed for the lifetime of the system. Future devices could make these parameters variable. Additionally or alternatively, virtualization could be employed to project multiple decoy systems to confuse attackers and to frequently roll back actual systems to a known good state in order to obviate

- **Collaborative**. Having the ability to work in partnership with other participants to collect and assess security information, and select, formulate, or alter an ACOA intended to counter an attack or sustain priority services.

- **Heterogeneous.** Having the ability to collaborate with other participants using a common communications channel despite differences in affiliation, security policies or service level agreements.

- **Diversifying.** Having the ability to sense the appearance or persona of surrounding devices and to make oneself different from other devices.

- **Resilient.** For cyber defense purposes, having sufficient capacity to simultaneously collect or receive and assess security information, execute any ACOA, make alterations to the ACOA as needed, and sustain agreed upon service levels.

- **Trustworthy.** Performing as expected – and only as expected – despite environmental disruption, user and operator errors, and attacks by hostile parties. Three approaches for achieving trustworthiness are software assurance[22], hardware enabled trust (e.g., Trusted Computing Group-based technologies, associated system architectures such as Network Admission Control or Trusted Network Connection and trusted virtualization) and data provenance (e.g., metadata tags and labels containing identity, origin, and transformation history).

"Unhealthy" information exchanges should be expensive or difficult to adapt. Or they might be easily compromised, disrupted, or corrupted. "Healthy" information exchanges are:

- **Secure**. Secure exchanges are those in which the identities of all participants in an exchange are authenticated, appropriate digital identities and minimum attribute data are asserted, and the vulnerability of any communications in the exchange to unauthorized interception, diversion, access, use, modification or disclosure is minimized[23].

- **Environmentally Sustainable.** Environmentally-sustainable exchanges are structured for the most rational use of cyber resources (least effort), are bandwidth friendly, easy to administer, and easy to achieve (for example, are broadly incorporated into commercial solutions).

- **Rapidly customizable.** Rapidly-customizable exchanges are enabled by user-configurable profiles, parameters and rules and by open application programming interfaces (APIs).

---

[22] DHS Software Assurance Program, https://buildsecurityin.us-cert.gov/swa/
[23] National Strategy for Trusted Identities in Cyberspace (NSTIC)

- **Lightweight and loosely coupled.** Lightweight and loosely-coupled exchanges are those that are achievable with existing infrastructure and with minor upgrades to existing tools and services, rather than through approaches that require extensive redesign.

Ecosystem-generated value, desired ecosystem and participant attributes, and ecosystem building blocks all work together. For example, an ecosystem with the ability to make automated adjustments to configuration in response to trust choices would offer increased reliability and resilience for supported business, social and civic processes while improving the privacy and civil liberties of users. An ecosystem with such abilities would also be self-defending. A self-defending ecosystem with human involvement could force attackers to take more risks and be more exposed. These activities, combined with greater attribution, could enable law enforcement or other deterrence to be more effective. A healthy ecosystem, in other words, mutually reinforces security, usability, reliability, and the protection of privacy and civil liberties.

Incentives and Adoption

We know today that users are not routinely complying with cyber best practices and configuration guidelines. Adoption of security standards is decidedly slow, and early indications are that cybersecurity continuous monitoring will face impediments to adoption. This indicates an imbalance of incentives, whereby defenders are not incented, but attackers are.

A persistent challenge in today's ecosystem is the inability to establish level of harm as a result of a cyber incident – be it loss of intellectual property, privacy, consumer confidence, business opportunity, or essential services. Such inability may be due in part to a lack of agreement on how to establish extent in a highly-interconnected environment as well as how to measure, validate, and communicate effects. It may also be due in part to a lack of trust, which impedes information sharing and collaboration.

Earlier, this paper proposed types of activities that might be associated with an appropriately automated and distributed "Cyber CDC" that performs threat and incident watch, data dissemination, threat analysis, intervention analysis and recommendations, and coordination of preventive actions. In addition to promoting cyber health among communities, such a capability could provide vendors and system owners with the information and insight needed to diagnose problems and evaluate options for new or improved capabilities. One way to get started is through increased sharing of anonymized cyber incident and mitigation data. Aggregation and analysis of such data might lead to an improved ability to show how investments in cyber health can reduce operating costs, improve business agility, or avoid extensive mitigation costs (e.g., the cost of data leakage protection software compared with the cost of mitigating large-scale identity information disclosure). Such insights would likely strengthen consumer demand for healthy products and services and reduce risks to participants.

Way Ahead

While this paper has presented a comprehensive view of a healthy cyber ecosystem, there are many open questions. On the more technical side, they include: Can the ongoing work on security content automation be repurposed for self defense? Will commercial products conform to open standards? To what extent can focus, convergence, and agility be decentralized to cyber systems in an autonomic (i.e., self-managing) fashion? Can autonomic defenses scale to encompass large-scale, distributed and multi-domain environments (e.g., mobile telephony, IP-based networks, and computing platforms), and if so, what elements of trust would be required?

Moreover, the path to successful realization is unclear. What are the business drivers that will incent the necessary investments? What are the appropriate roles and responsibilities of the public and private sector in delivering the healthy ecosystem? Which elements should be prioritized for early realization?

As a healthy cyber ecosystem emerges, governance questions become salient. Will system owners cede decision making to the community? Who sets policy for inter-enterprise information exchange and deployment of countermeasures? What liability regimes apply for collateral consequences of countermeasure deployment (or the failure to deploy known countermeasures)? What legal authorities should local and national governments, as well as international entities, have to compel action by devices owned by or serving private parties in order to secure the larger cyber commons?

Clearly the field is ripe for planning and action. The authors welcome feedback on this paper, and comment on all aspects of the problem. We are continuing our own analysis, and we plan to publish our findings, together with your feedback (to cyberfeedback@dhs.gov), in a sequel paper and a proposed action plan that, at a minimum, identifies key game-changing initiatives for each of the three building blocks. Potential game-changing initiatives might include:

- Piloting, demonstration, and rapid promulgation of community and inter-community ACOAs for collective defense

- Piloting, demonstration, and rapid promulgation of security content automation standards for functions described in the second and third waves of Figure 5

- Building upon the draft NSTIC to achieve standards-based device authentication, including small and often wireless devices composing massively scalable grids.

Glossary

General Terms

- **Cyber devices** is a general term used to refer to computers; software systems, applications or services; electronic communications systems, networks, or services; and the information contained therein.

- **Cyber participants** refers to people, processes, and devices.

- **Information structuring** refers to methods and standards that organize data into components and relationships. A general example of structured information is a United States address. Its components are street number, street name, city, state, and zip code. States have fixed two-digit code names and zip codes have a specified five- or nine-digit format. An example of structured cyber security information is Common Platform Enumeration (CPE), a naming scheme for some elements of cyber systems. The top-level components of a CPE are platform name, hardware parts, operating system parts, and application parts. Structured cyber security information is necessary to automate activities that identify and manage cyber devices and their components, describe and manage security configurations and vulnerabilities, identify and track attackers and attack tools (e.g., malicious code or botnets), detect and describe events and attacks, express and execute cyber security policies or courses of action, describe and provide notice of cyber posture, and so on.

- **Cyber information exchange** refers to sharing relationships and protocols that allow cyber participants to publish and subscribe, signal, or request and respond with cyber security information using consistent semantics.

Standards Acronyms

ARF	Assessment Results Format
CAIF	Common Announcement Interchange Format
CAPEC	Common Attack Pattern Enumeration and Classification
CCE	Common Configuration Enumeration
CEE	Common Event Expression
CPE	Common Platform Enumeration
CVE	Common Vulnerabilities and Exposures
CVSS	Common Vulnerability Scoring System
CWE	Common Weakness Enumeration
IDMEF	Intrusion Detection Message Exchange Format
IODEF	Incident Object Description and Exchange Format
MAEC	Malware Attribute Enumeration and Characterization
NIEM	National Information Exchange Model
OVAL	Open Vulnerability and Assessment Language
SecDEF	Security Description and Exchange Format
XCCDF	Extensible Configuration Checklist Description Format